tiptoe and whisper

janaya martin

janaya martin

janaya arellano
2024

ISBN 978-1-63489-027-4
eISBN 978-1-63489-026-7

Library of Congress Catalog Number: 2015960987
Printed in the United States of America
First Printing: 2016
20   19   18   17   16   5   4   3   2   1

Cover design by Jessie Bright

Wise Ink Creative Publishing
837 Glenwood Ave.
Minneapolis, MN 55405
www.wiseinkpub.com

To order, visit www.itascabooks.com or call 1-800-901-3480.
Reseller discounts available.

tiptoe
and
whisper

janaya martin

For Sarah —

This is what I
get for opening
my big mouth!
Not my best
work, but my book baby
nonetheless. ♡ Janaya

WISE
CREATIVE ★ PUBLISHING
Ink
est. 2012

This book is for my thirteen-year-old self—
I told you you'd make it—and for my children,
who are the perfect combination of magic and mischief.

Also, for Sherrie Fernandez-Williams
for always being that friend.

table of

contents

For Tom

You were kind and soft
when others were not
you may have wanted from me
all the things they did
but you never let it slip
I could be a girl around you
without having to worry too much
about what that could mean.
You would read my poems
and let me read yours.
Once
we wandered the city all night
we wrote dreams on small slips of paper
and planted them in trees
set them to sail on the river.

You let them get you.
They stuck their claws right into your sweetness,
and one night,
years later,
our eyes met
and I could see you were already gone . . .

Letters

I can't slam.
My poems are never long enough
or deep enough.
I'm too simple for the complexities
of poetry.

I am not a poet.
The title was given to me.
It was part of
my classification.
The result of someone
trying to mold me.

I don't even write poetry.
I write letters to you.
I stamp them and
I mail them.
In a way.

Before you, I wrote letters
to him and before him,
my father.

Before the letters to my father
there were only stories.
Short ones.

There was the one about my
great-grandma and buying pants.
They wanted it in the paper.

It never made it to the paper.

I never made it to you.
I am not a poet any more than this is a poem.

I am a girl writing letters.
I am a woman waiting
for a reply.

What It Means to Be a Woman

I don't know how many
times I woke up to the sound
of my mother screaming.
I only remember wondering
why she thought I could save her.

I was the one who needed saving.
I was the one who needed sleep,
but there she was again, in my
room, hoping that I could stop
his fists.

I couldn't.

I don't know how many
men have hit my mother.
I just know that it has been too many.

I was nine years old when
I learned the word rape
and that it was my mom's fault
for being drunk and alone
in a bar parking lot.

I was ten years old when
I got my period for the first time.
I had no idea what was happening.
I showed my mom and she started bawling.
I thought I was dying.

She said, "You're a woman now."
I thought she must have this
all wrong.
I wasn't even good at being a kid.
I certainly wasn't ready to be a woman.

I'm still not ready.

Anchored

These days, when I wake up,
I already feel like
I've had six cups of coffee.

My stomach twisted
and uneasy.

Anxiety.

I live here now.

Treading the line of *everything is going to be okay,*
and *everything is fucked.*

I used to be your drum. I wonder too often
if you remember that.
You made me smile
in a way that felt like a surprise
every time.

I want to stop remembering the way
your hands felt
against my thighs,
the way your eyes always seem
to be saying more than your lips ever will.
I want you to call me
in the middle of the night
to tell me you had that dream too.

I want to stop putting every man in my life
in your shadow.
I want to stop craving your light.

I want my love poems to stop calling you home.
I want the basement to flood
and the walls to mold.

I want it to be too dangerous for me to come here,

year after year,

line after line.

Tiptoe and Whisper

Tiptoe down the hallway
of your childhood
only to find all of the
cupboards empty
picture frames missing memories
ashtrays spilling over
tables littered with beer bottles,
Zig-Zags and roach clips
and the TV always on.

Whisper to the shadows
that it will be okay
you will grow up
you will not make the same mistakes
and it will be over soon.

Some Days Are Better Than Others

They say, "No sleep for the wicked."
Well, I must be as wicked as they come.
The void is in my hair
stuck under my nails
and I can't seem to rid
myself of it.
Can't shit or piss it out
can't wash it from my skin.

I'm better lost than found,
most days it seems.
Thoughts flashing in and out
like fireflies
as my fingers hover over the keys
aching for just that one line,
that one line that will make
it all worthwhile.

No scream loud enough.
No silence quiet enough.
Never enough.

I butt my last cigarette
and wish myself luck,
luck,
luck.

Something Bigger

I've never quite figured out
what is wrong with my mother.

My finger always hovering
somewhere between her head
and chest.

Too often I have imagined
my beginning independent
of flesh, aching to
be the product of something
more permanent.

Something bigger than a murdered father
reduced to ash and memory,
bigger than
an alcoholic mother
stuck on an adolescent loop.

Both of them humming like a
tired fluorescent light at the edge of my life,
illuminating my limits.

Their shadows desperate and looming over
every move I make
only letting me get so far away
before my face reminds me—
these eyes are my mother's,
these lips are my father's,
but the things I see and
the words I speak
are all my own.

Hungry

I used to play poet

so many words

in so many columns.

So many lines lacking proper punctuation.

I thought I was doing it right

if I was doing it wrong.

But the rejection slips keep piling up

against the great praise of

people who can't write me checks.

I keep this job

so I can eat

but my heart is on fire

and my fingers are aching.

Thirsty

I remember standing out in the rain
and watching a bead
of water roll down
the slope of your nose
and holding back
when my tongue wanted
nothing more than to
catch it before it fell.

Your face makes me thirsty
and this cup is never empty
you spill in and over the top

and I drink
and I drink

with no relief.

Stumble

I keep your picture in my living room;
it helps me to remember
how much I have forgotten
over the years,
how much I have let slip away,
almost unnoticed.

On these nights when I am
lulled by the passing of cars
on the freeway, I stumble to the
shelf where you are kept
and hold you in my hands
as if it means something.

Nine months have passed
and your absence still bleeds
and I am still looking for you
at each bus stop I pass
on my way to work and on
my way home.

We still have coffee together,
you and I, but there
is no laughter as there once was.
There is no hello or goodbye.
There is just me
and the steam
rising from the cup in
my hands.

Switchblade

Soft-spoken white ladies
write poems about the ocean
and flowers and birds.

How precious.

I come to the page like the thief of joy
killing all hope that you'll
come away okay.

I don't have shit to lose
or prove.

Roofers

There are shingles in the trees
and nails on the ground
caution tape flapping in the wind
like the fading evidence
that a crime has been committed.

There are men overdressed
for this high sun
pounding and pounding,
and it hurts my head.
They are scurrying around,
frantic, speaking
a language I don't understand.

I am smoking
and typing
and drinking coffee.
Each time I suck
the smoke in, it hurts.

My mouth tastes like
seventh grade, eager
and confused,
waiting for reprieve.

Relevance

There was a time
when we made sense
to each other.

A time when
we had nothing
but time
and we shared
moments
that seemed
to carry
and made memories
that tasted sweet.

Now,
alone in this room
with nothing but
thoughts of you,
my mouth is dry
with bitterness.

I want you
to take it back
just so you can
give it again.

I want you
to see me
cracked open
like the pages
of these poems,
touch the ink
and feel the relevance.

Quit It Out

You don't remember
the time I took a $40 cab
ride to your house, because when I
arrived—you were not there.

You were out stepping on toes
and chasing the wind.
I stumbled to the door
and sprinkled words against
the air you left behind.

I was crazy in ways
that have not left me.
I guess that means that I
am crazy still.

I wish I could make you remember
that I was good once and you were too.

Low Glow

in the low glow from the bed table lamp
her face looked softer than
she'd seen it in months
her laugh lines deeper than the furrow of her brow
she seemed closer to happy

yet she was lonely
she ached to have someone to
pull close against her
someone that was just as empty

someone who could admire
the deep curve of her spine
with fingertips as gentle
as whisper

Heroin Is Bad

You were scattered
across the patio.
All of your pieces
hit me at once,
and I cried as they ran
fingers across you.

I took what I could
stand to take
but for reasons
beyond taking.

What's done is not done.
You weren't finished yet
and neither was I.

Isolation

He went on to live
with women who made
him feel something I
could not, women
who knew more about
broken than my tiny
remnants ever would.

I went on to live
with ghosts, forced
to chase his shadow.
Aching for a sign
that the end was near,
but there is no end.
Only the beginning
of a beginning
again and again.

Grace

My neck remembers your breath,
the way it spiraled like smoke
against my flesh
in that tender place between
shoulder and skull.
I find myself too often
tracing the years
with restless fingertips
taking tally with scars
and wrinkles.
There is no use keeping track
of where you dare not tread,
as your fears will find you
off guard, and your memories
will not save you.
Your heroes are not heroic
and the last leg of the race
is all your own, so pen the petty
mighty and call it a day.

Gesture

Smoking beneath a starless sky,
waiting "with a glacier's patience"
for my turn to roll back around.
In the distance there is light,
proof that another day has
yet to come. Still, I have no space for sleep,
as you incessantly find me there.
You hold me loosely
with your words
while your eyes tempt me and your
hands let me slip through.
I wake to the sound of my breath
repentant and labored
palms sweaty, lips dry.
I rise with the fall of our story
and curse the sky with
hand gestures
because my throat is tired
and there is no use for words
when they can't bring you home.

Draw

I am at the center
of where it all began.
I am drawing lines
and circles
around memories.

I am thumbing pages
and creating new chapters,
yet the story remains the same.

I am afraid that high noon
has come to pass
and as we got to ten,
my gun jammed.

You walked your paces
and I walked mine . . .
we turned at the same time
and for a moment
there was hope
until there was no hope at all.

Grown-up has no room
for do-overs, but I'm
doing it all over,
at the center of where
it all began.

Dirty

Lips parted

this sigh ricochets
off of empty space
when once upon
a time your hands
were the period at the
end of my dirty thoughts.

Every step succeeded by
longing with nowhere to go.

Broken

This body
is just
a body,
a house without walls,
and I keep thinking that maybe
just maybe
if I ask nicely
you will work
your way in.

I feel sometimes
like the woman who sang,
"Enough is not enough
without more."

Still, I will not ask you to stay
if you come
or return
if you go.

I will not trouble you
with my words
or my memories.
I will simply ask nicely,
"Just once?"

Dirge

I want there to be silence here.
In that space between my ears
where my brain once was
and knew what it was doing;
that space between my heart and my mouth
where a soul once lived.

How many times have I needed
to tell you goodbye?
And how many times have I seen
that look on your face?
Those eyes that make me feel like sticking my hand
in a meat grinder would be better than this.

I am again picking him over you.

You, one of the greatest friends I've ever had.
You, who wrote me into your poems
and made me the star of your stories.
You, who drove twenty-some hours straight
just to tell me in your own kind of way
that you love me and that you always have.

I remember picking blades of grass from my clothes last
summer, I remember leaving mascara marks on your sweater,
I remember those talks down by the river.
And yet, the only thing I have left to say to you is:
goodbye.

The First

He used to tiptoe through strangers' houses
high and bold
fingering gold coins and jewelry
sometimes pausing in the moment to watch them sleeping
as their chests rose and fell.

He used to touch me
before I was ready
because my face told him otherwise.
He kissed me under a bridge when I was twelve.
His tongue was like an answered prayer,
my body instantaneously alive with all of
the stuff I never understood
while sneaking peeks at my stepdad's Playboy.

When he dumped me, I cried for three days straight.
My mother tried to console me, but I heard her
cry some nights too over a broken heart
older than me.

I didn't understand the power of first love
until I saw him again, seventeen years later.
There he was outside my apartment door
at twelve a.m.
I watched him through the peephole
for too long before opening the door
wishing he'd changed, wishing he was fat
or ugly or both.

As he came in, I hugged him,
my heart leaping out of my chest,
landing against his,

and I couldn't let go.

I finally understood what it felt like
to come home.

You Promised

You leave me with this book full of words you didn't write.
You say that everything written here
reminds you of me,
but what it reminds me of
is how many times I thought someone loved me
and I let them write me someone else's letters,
how many times I let them sing me someone else's songs.
What it reminds me of
are the countless pages
you promised.

Meanwhile I am writing in blood.
I am playing for keeps
with the spiders and the dust bunnies
and all of the nothing you left behind.

You left me here
with this book in my hands
and I can't read it.
I can't read Anis's words
like they are meant for me.
I don't know his hands.
I didn't love his hands.
I loved you. I love you.

I realized today that I have never
really loved anyone before you.
I lived in fairytales,
I lived in movie scripts.
I lived in beer bottles and ashtrays
and I lived in
"I guess this is good enough."

But you.

You were the light that God made.
You are every breath I take in
and every sigh I let out.
You are the alphabet strung together
to form this howl in my gut.

You.
You asked me to never stop
writing to you,
but I will.
I have.
I love me more than you,
so this is a letter to me.
These are my words
and this is my love
and I owe it to myself
to be better than this.

I owe it to myself to say
"Fuck you!"
and mean it.
You broke me
but I am not broken.
I am pieces on the mend.

Origin

I am from the changing seasons
that last too long or not long enough.
I am from wind and rain, sun and rainbows.
I am from crunching leaves,
snowflakes, and icicles.

I am from outspoken women laughing,
from men who leave, from children
running through sprinklers and alleyways.

I am from saying grace over gravy and potatoes,
and holding back laughter or getting "the eye."
I am from turkey and baked green beans and
never-ending sweets.

I am from spirit plates and tobacco,
from Jesus and redemption,
from It is what it is
and Don't worry, you'll get there.

I am from the lost and I am from the found.
I am from words overflowing
and lips locking under bridges and in cars.

I am from a series of rooms
without roots, a book of
faces without names.

I am from pain and inspiration.
Where are you from?

Tell Me

I want to believe that no one has been inside you the way I
have.
That no one has twisted you up quite like me.
That no one has crawled under your skin or picked your scabs
just to lick them clean again
like I have
I want to believe that you have never been so angry
or hurt or alive or full of hope like you have been
with me.
In the dark, our skin damp and limbs twisted
I thought I knew what love was, but I had it all wrong.
Love is not patient or kind or sweet or soft.
It is hard and mean and abrupt.
They tell me you are wrong for me,
that you cannot be forgiven,
they tell me I deserve better,
more.
How would they know?
How could they possibly know what I need,
what I deserve?
You have always known me,
and I have always known you.
This was always happening.
And I am not who they think I am.

Doe-Eyed and Perfect

All of my best poems are about you
and all of my worst ones too.

It's funny when I sit
and think about how much
space I have allowed you to occupy
inside me, how many pens have gone dry
trying to convince you

and me

that this love
is the best thing for you

and me.

All the while, I don't even know you.

I met you seventeen years ago
on a sidewalk outside of our sober high school
you had a mustache and I was deep in the
trenches of how foreign my life had become.

City girl moved to the suburbs, no longer
allowed to wander and smoke weed—
every night and every day having to face
myself and the fact that both of my
parents had left me in one way or another

But there you were
all doe-eyed and perfect.

For Quinten

Your father had a tongue
that spoke
two languages at once.
Unfortunately, I misunderstood
both of them.

There was little to agree on
in the end
and it came so soon,

the end

rushing up against me
like a flood,

the earth's entire
water supply
lapping at my toes
and my knees,
every ocean, stream, lake,
and river eventually overtaking
my lungs.

I couldn't breathe, but
in the end
there was you.

In Search of My Mother's Smile

I stumbled upon my own

fashioned out of longing and

regret

yellowed and gummy

lacking a statement

as if my mouth

knew my story before

I

could say the words

before I

could write it down

     in pencil

and erase

the parts that scared me:

     violence.

        sadness.

          death.

If I Had Written Nothing

You are gone now.
I watched you drive away.
I stood in the door
beneath the clouds
and my regret
behind my sunglasses
and watched
you
drive
away.

I let you leave
and now I am here holding the
silence in two hands.
I am holding your absence
in the center of who I
was before you left.

You asked if I had anything to say to you
and the answer is yes.
Yes, I have everything to say to you.
I have the cold October breeze to say,
the falling leaves, the sun
hiding behind the clouds.
I have labored heartbeats and
streaming tears to tell you.

I have years of hope
and forgotten dreams
to translate.

None of this matters now.

I watched you drive away.
I let you leave.
My limbs tried to fight for you,
my lips tried to tell you,
I saw our little boy
yesterday.
He was you
and he was me.

He and I are ghosts now,
haunting each other
reminding the sky of what
might have been
If I had
written you nothing.

Snippets

There are four voices travelling
the hall—two children, girls,
politely answering the questions
of two prying adults, a
man and a woman.
The children traveled
to Rome and Venice this summer.
I'm envious.
Their father is a kind man
who has never mispronounced my name.
The woman tells him that the children
have been horseback riding.
I hear him say he loves going
to the horse barn at the state fair
and I smile to myself
because all I can recall
is how awful it smells.
His face reminds me of a man
I loved once, a man I love still
in the quiet way you do
when things are meant to be settled.

Simple

Tonight I smell the way I smelled with you:
tired, like I spent all day searching.
And I have.
I don't miss your voice.
I am comfortable with this silence
and I don't miss you,
but as I lay across this bed in the dark
I feel that there is too much space
for one person to fill.

Gravity

Do not be mistaken.
When all is said and done,
it is still your name upon my lips.
Reason insists, however,
that I untie this knot,
myself from you.

My love has taken flight.
I've released it into the sky
and my arms struggle
to stay at my sides.

My resolve is always strong
in the beginning.
Peacefully I watch
all that love released,
floating away from me
until memory takes over.
Then the air begins to slowly escape,
and it all comes falling down around me.

It is no longer the memory of moments
that grip me,
but rather the memory of feeling.
I miss feeling.

I miss the dizziness of anticipation,
the recklessness of desire,
the weightlessness of succumbing
to all that you could ever need
right there, in that moment.

I miss the ease of a returned embrace,
the quick exchange of breath,
quietly telling me there is
no need to retreat.

Reason insists, however,
that I untie this knot,
myself from you.

Claws Out

I am not beautiful.

I am always talking
about the lack of breath
and the weight of years.

The truth is quite simple,
it is your weight that I crave.
I have become consumed with the
need to feel it upon me.

When the nights are slow and lonely
you come to me in ways that
don't make sense, and I am used up
and left to fend off the need for more.

It is not beautiful.

Desire is ugly and I
want to be done with it.
I want to be done with
the need for you
and the lies I've told myself
to avoid the pain of moments
without return.

You Are Mount Everest

the noise in the ceiling has started again
the wallpaper hates me
and I have nowhere to go
I have died in this room
year after year
and the spirit of the girl
we used to love
still fights me for this body.
I have been lured in by
blades of grass ,
loved by semi-trucks and mountains
I was too afraid to climb.

Toothache

They're going to find me here
in my tacky pajamas,
purple shorts and green T-shirt
dressed like the joker
smeared eye make up
face swollen from
infection, drool crusted
in the corners of my mouth.

Yes, they are going to
find me here
in my mess of a room
filled to the brim
with clothing and
books and an open
laptop with these words
across the screen.

Possibility

I felt it swirling there for years
and failed to make mention.
It began at my feet as I
walked and walked,
both away from and toward
people and things and memories.
It settled in my knees
for a time until my age
said, ""Ha! This is no age at all!""
and it kept on.
It found a place in my hips
and I remembered all the ways in
which I am human and female
and beautiful and hungry.
It slithered up my spine
making my heart and
my lungs come alive.
It came to my lips
and transformed.
I said it aloud,
I smiled and it was
returned to me.

Persistence leads to possibility
and here I am
dancing again.

That Time I Cried

I saw a dead cat on
the road today—

its fur wet
and matted—

I wanted to cry
but couldn't.
I was distracted by
my own
fleeting moments
and the rain coming down,
occasionally still
in the form of a snowflake.

I wanted to turn
around and crawl back
into bed.

I wanted to crawl
back into summer,
to that moment when
I knew I loved you.

We hadn't said more than
a few words to each other,
but you made a tiny
ice cream cone for Olive
and it was perfect.

You were perfect
and I couldn't speak.

I left that night
wondering where
the world was taking me
when I saw a dead raccoon
on the road,
and, that time, I cried.

These Shoes

Already I have worn through the soles
of these shoes. Already my toes
are swollen and I am two-stepping
with the madness of desire.

I hear the names of children I have never met
as I rise each morning. I see their tiny
faces in the sun and hear their laughter in the breeze.

If you ask without desperation,
the Universe is always happy to oblige.
So keep your tongue quiet
until you are truly able to receive,
or you will look down
and see your feet in someone else's shoes.

Maybe The Dead Can Travel

The rain looks like snow falling:
slow and lazy.
I guess I'm used to rain being more eager to
get where it's going.
It's almost two a.m.
and I wonder where you are.
As if you're still traveling,
as if the dead have places to be.
Each time the lightning flashes,
the light spreads across the sky
like the veins in my chest,
like lines across a map.
I expect your face to be illuminated.
It is not and I feel magnified
with each flash and then
emptied, removed, less
a part of what I was moments before.

July 22

This day holds significance
and I can't place my finger
on the reason(s) why.

I woke up twelve minutes late for work,
an hour behind schedule
and I stumbled around in circles
not knowing exactly what to do.

And then I found the coffee
and I smelled you in the air.

This day unfolds with diligence
and I can't stop my hands
from finding my face
or the memories from finding
their
way
in.

Yes, I still have some things
I would like to say to you
but I lack grace
and you lack time.

End

Five birds gathered in the yard
the morning you left.
They pecked at the dead grass,
looking for something.

I didn't watch you walk out the door
and I didn't watch you drive away.

Instead I watched the silver maple sway
in the wind. I counted
the branches that had already
fallen—there were four.
I remembered the
night I woke you up because I
didn't know that what I heard
was just rain and not war.

You got me back to sleep,
with whispers,
your arms locked
tightly around me.
I was comforted still by the breath
of your lies against my hair and my neck.

I am thinking now of the way I danced
around our truth as the distance
between us grew
and grew until there was a valley
so wide all I could do was
cry into it and sail away.

Hands

I've been thinking about your hands.
In my mind, I've been holding them
against my own
and marveling at the contrast.
Your hands do not show your age,
only your nerve, your fears.
Your skin is smooth and brown
and sure of where it belongs,
protecting your blood
and your bones.

I think about the strength
they possess and how you
don't seem to notice.
Your hands, at the ends
of your arms, an
extension of the hope
inside your chest.

Your hands framing my face,
your fingers penning a letter.

I have always been able to
remember your hands.
I have often wondered
about the women
they've touched,
the words they've written, and
the doors
they've opened
and closed. ´

With Social Skills Stuck on Stutter

I never know where to put my hands
when I don't have pockets.
I tend to touch my face
and cover my mouth.
I have this problem with smiling
too often
and speaking too soon.

I never know where to rest my eyes.,
They're always trying to find a way
into the places they don't belong.

I've never been very good with people,
they make me nervous, and
when I'm nervous I just
want to run.

Thing is, people are lazy
and no longer willing to give chase.
Or perhaps
I fail to inspire.

I drove home after the party
completely engrossed in
my aloneness when
I saw a raccoon dead on the road.
I cried.
I cried for him.
I cried for me.

I too am lying lifeless
on life's road

eyes blank
and glazed
waiting for someone
or something
to scoop me up and
breathe a little life
back into me.

You're Welcome

When it's cold like this
and I can see my breath
there is no denying
that I am alive
but I keep wanting to
hold it in
till it hurts
because
that makes sense to me.

I tried to avoid the St. Paul skyline
tried to ignore the clock ticking
the seconds,
the distance,
tried to think
of
what not to say
how
not to look . . .
a life so long—somehow too short
a love so big—still too small

When I see you
I
miss
me.

I didn't spit in your coffee.

You're welcome.

Out in the Open

I have come to this place before.
I have sat among these thoughts
and gathered these decisions in my hands
like fruit.
I have tasted each one separately
and chosen to walk back to the place I began
and offer them back to the trees
from which they fell.

Slowly,
intentionally,
I am becoming the woman
I was meant to be.

Beast

It happens too often,
we are taken against our will
by the weightlessness of
fingertips and whispers
and the minutes press
upon each other
equally wanting to and not wanting
to break free.

My father's face comes to me
sometimes, but that is all.
I do not know his voice or his words.
I do not know the strength of his arms
or his will.
His face comes to me early in the morning
when I am wiping the sleep from
my eyes and trying to make sense
of the day.

As I gain focus
he is there looking back at me,
in freckles and spirited brow,
in lower lip and
devil's tongue.

Each December,
as a new year approaches,
I am painfully aware of what
I have lost and gained
with the shadow
of his memory
hanging silently
over me.

Dusty

The memories are fading
and I can no longer trust my recollections.
I know your name and I know your face,
but there are places you have been
that I have never seen,
stories you've written
in a tongue I don't understand.

I sometimes turn those
youthful years
in my hands,
smoothing the edges,
reworking the clay,
but time is fleeting
and time pulls
at my corners
till all I can do is walk away.

Still, I wonder
as my hand brushes the dust
from the place I have saved for you,
what it is about you—
a beautiful stranger—
that keeps my hope alive.

Truths

I have one thousand stories
inside my mouth, in my gut, my heart, my toes.
You are the main character these days.

I have one-act plays waiting
between my hips.

I have swing dance moves behind each knee.

When you look at me, I am a spool of
thread unraveling, one kiss at a time.
When I look at you,
I see the clumsy teenage boy you were
falling out of my bedroom window,
hoping my uncle wouldn't catch you.

When I look at you as a man,
I am weak and I am cautious.

I wonder what it is we think we're doing.

I wonder.

Daycare

I was trying to tell my son I loved him.
He was looking at me with those big, curious eyes
and they communicated to me that he knew,
though the words never left his mouth.
The words never leave his mouth.
At seventeen months old, everyone is concerned that he isn't
talking.
He isn't talking.

Why isn't your son talking?

Why isn't my son talking?

There was a little girl on the couch,
her white-blonde hair framing her face
and I was trying to tell my son that I loved him
and she said to me, "I have horses on my shirt"
and I said, "Cool, I like horses," but that is a half-truth.
I don't know enough about horses to know if I like them.
I've never ridden a horse
I've never touched a horse
I've only seen them in stalls at the state fair
with their butts facing the people and sad, sad eyes.
I've only seen them in movies
where people are being exploited again and again and again.

Then a little boy says, "I have letters on my shirt."
I say, "Yes and numbers too."
I think of all of the boys who grow
up into angry men and live in cages
as numbers, no longer letters
or names or people or human.

I look at my son,
he is holding two trucks.
I want him to tell me a story.

Another little boy yells at me,
but I can't make out the words.
He's so excited and looks down.
He has a dinosaur on his shirt.

The little girl tells me she's going to the dentist
and I try to keep myself from scrunching
up my face, but I fail
so I try to distract her with words
as she has distracted me with words
and say, "Dentists are very nice."

My Father's Ghost

Each night I hear you coming,
like a soft breeze through
the first-floor window my
mother always warned me to close.

I'm not scared anymore.
Your footsteps are in rhythm
to my breath or my heartbeat.
I trace your path with eyes closed.

I remember when you left
but not as clearly as
your return.

The sun shone through the blinds,
leaving a slatted pattern on the wall.
My belly was growing and I watched
dust dance and float in the air.

You paced my room while I slept.
Each morning I woke up heavier,
sadness thick at the back of my throat
like a sickness you can't undo.

That's what death does,
even twenty years later.
It hangs, it settles,
it tickles and teases,
and your ghost is a cruel trick
that still never manages to let me
let go of you.

Patricia Smith

I watched you carefully,
glasses on, glasses off.

Behind the podium
effortless and booming.
Poem after poem
cutting me open and
cracking ribs.

I have been changed.

From the back of the room
I claimed you as my mother.
The one I never had
but wanted.
The one who tells me
how poems speak.
The one who says
we have two throats.
I meant to ask you about trust,
but I don't trust myself
to speak aloud in public.
I tell myself too often
not to ask questions.

I have been changed.

I would like to stand
hushed against a wall
in your home,
to hear the conversations
between you and your husband
about the pages you've written.

Growing up, I searched
for women like you.
Women whose voices
carried, women who
saw what the world was doing to us
but marched on anyway,
writing it down, saying it aloud.

I Don't Matter

My body is ash.
My body is dust.
My body is what is left after
your limbs refused to bend
around me.

You told me once
that I was the kind of girl
you could marry
but my lips said "fuck" too much
and we fucked too much
and who was I anyway?

A pretty girl you met at a party,
some late-night chat over messenger?
Less than a month later
I was the vessel that would almost break
against your distance.
I was the fragile and damaged package
carrying your fourth child.

His fingerprints are laced,
his blood, sweet and tainted,
from all those nights I cried
and cradled my stomach alone
watching his limbs press and stretch
trying to make my womb his own.

acknowledgments

This book has been a long time coming, and as I reflect on all of the forces that needed to collide in order for a dream to become a reality, it is really nothing short of amazing. I am so blessed to have such talented, supportive, and appropriately pushy friends. A special thank you to Scott Martin, Lauren Kavan, Terri Wrobleski, and Melissa Thompson for being such strong supporters of this book.

A BIG shout-out to all of the other folks who supported this project in various ways, whether that was contributing to my fund-raising campaign, spreading the word on Facebook, or sending me words of encouragement along the way!

This book is my baby. It's true what they say: it takes a village. So thank you for being my village!